1 - Al-Wujood - Existence (Allah Exists)

Does Allah exist?

Yes He does! Of course He does!

How can we know if He exists?

"Just Look around! Look around!"

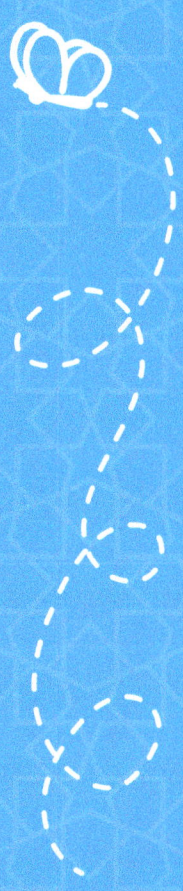

Didn't they make themselves?

No they didn't! That is impossible!

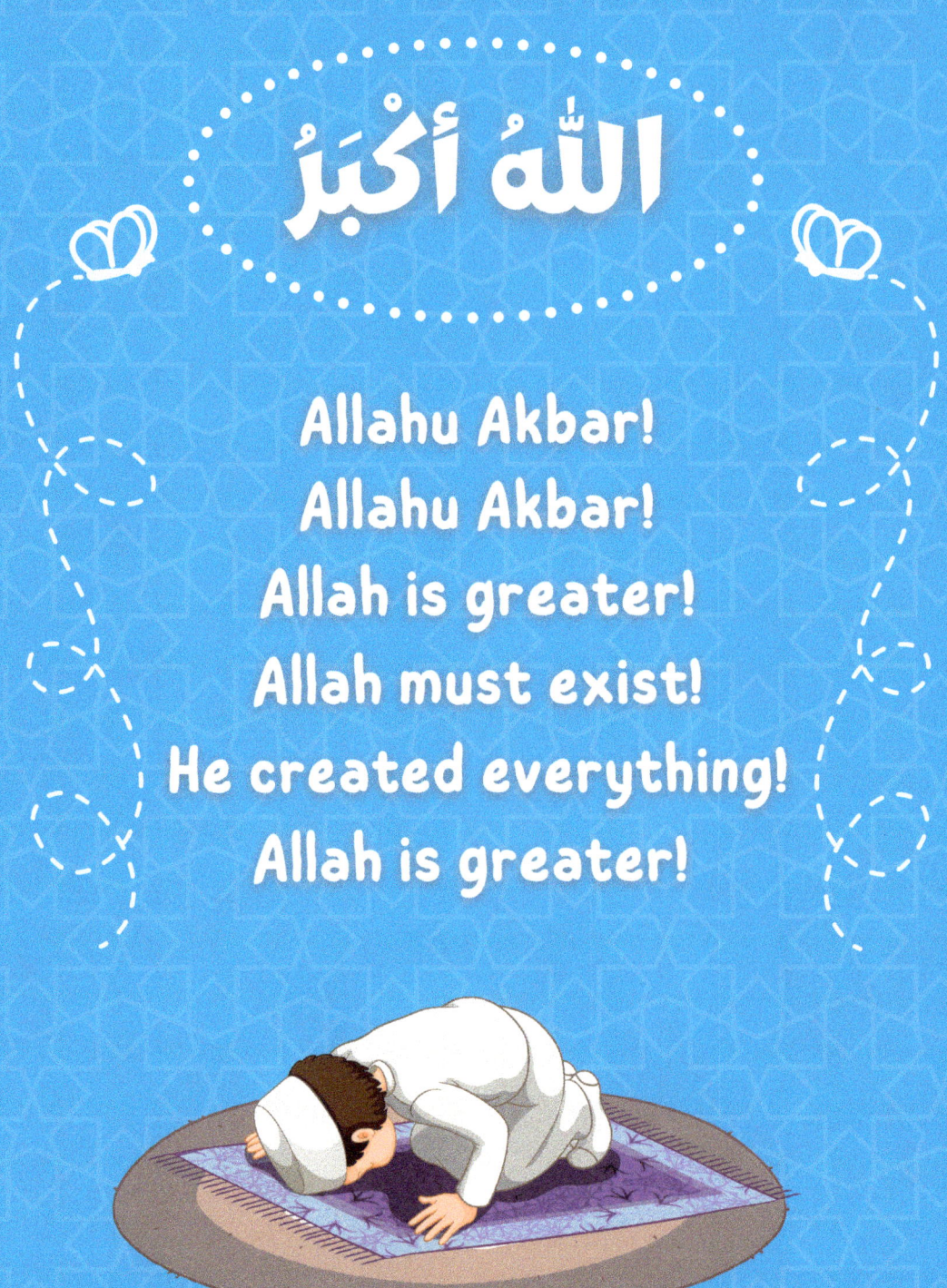

2 - Al-Qidam - Being Eternal (Allah is Eternal)

Does Allah have a beginning?

No He doesn't.
No He doesn't.

Is Allah First without beginning?

Yes He is.
Yes He is.

3 - Al-Baqa' - Everlastingness (Allah is Everlasting)

Does Allah have an ending?

No He Doesn't.
No He Doesn't.

Is Allah last without ending?

Yes He is.
Of course He is.

4 - Al-Mukhaalafah Lil-khalqi - Unlike His Creation In Any Way

Does Allah resemble anyone?

"No He doesn't. No He doesn't."

Does Allah resemble anything?

No He doesn't. Of course He doesn't.

Can we imagine Allah?

"No we can't. Of course we can't."

Can we know what Allah is?

"No we can't. Of course we can't."

Allahu Akbar!
Allahu Akbar!
Allah is greater!
Greater than creation
And imagination
Allah is greater!

Does Allah have a shape?

No He doesn't.
No He doesn't.

Does Allah have a size?

• • • • •

"No He doesn't,
Of course He doesn't."

Does Allah have any borders?

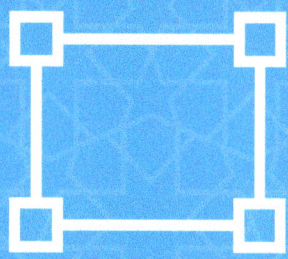

No He doesn't, No He doesn't.

Does Allah have a direction?

"No He doesn't, Of course He doesn't."

Allahu Akbar!
Allahu Akbar!
Allah is greater!
Greater than creation
And all limitations
Allah is greater!

5 - Al-Qiyam Bin-nafsi - Needs No One and Nothing

Does Allah need to sleep?

"No He doesn't, No He doesn't."

Does Allah need anyone?

No He Doesn't, No He doesn't.

اللهُ أَكْبَرُ

Allahu Akbar!
Allahu Akbar!
Allah is greater!
Allah is not in need
He's the sustainer
Allah is greater!

6 - Al-Wahdaniyyah - Oneness (Allah is One)

Is Allah more than One?

No He isn't.
No He isn't.

Is Allah made of parts?

No He isn't.
No He isn't.

Does Allah have any partners?

No He doesn't. Of course He doesn't.

7 - Al-Hayat - Life (Allah is Alive)

Is Allah alive?

الحَيّ
The Living One

"Yes He is. Yes He is"

Is it possible for Allah to die?

DE~~A~~TH

"No it's not. of course it's not."

8 - Al-Ilm - Knowledge (Allah Knows All)

Does Allah know everything?

Yes He does.
Yes He does.

اللهُ أَكْبَرُ

Allahu Akbar!
Allahu Akbar!
Allah is greater!
Allah is the living one
Allah knows everything
Allah is greater!

9 - Al-Iradah - Will (Allah's Power to Choose)

Does Allah choose what exists?

Yes He does.
Of course He does.

Does He choose what doesn't exist?

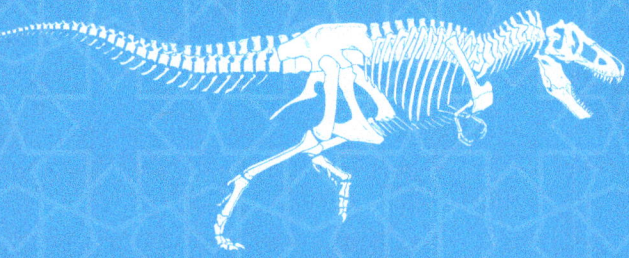

Yes He does.
Of course He does.

10 - Al-Qudrah - Allah's Power Over Everything

Can Allah make things exist?

Yes He can.
Of course He can.

Allahu Akbar!
Allahu Akbar!
Allah is greater!
Allah chooses what He likes
Allah does what He likes
Allah is greater!

11 - Al-Basar - Sight (Allah Sees All)

Does Allah see all things?

Yes He does.
Of course He does.

Without needing eyes to see?

> Yes He does.
> Of course He does.

11 - As-Sama' - Hearing (Allah Hears All)

Does Allah hear all things?

"Yes He does. Of course He does."

Without needing ears to hear?

Yes He does.
OF course He does.

اللهُ أكْبَرُ

Allahu Akbar!
Allahu Akbar!
Allah is greater!
Allah sees everything
Allah hears everything
Allah is greater!

13 - Al-Kalaam - Speech (Allah Speaks)

Does Allah also speak?

Yes He does. Of course He does.

Without a tongue, lips or cheeks?

Yes He does.
Of course He does.

Does He need a language to speak?

No He doesn't.
No He doesn't.

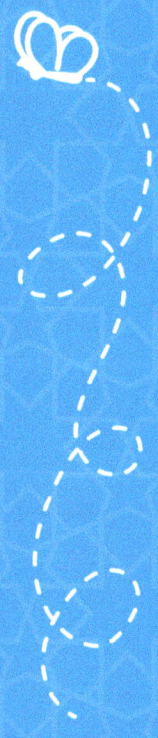

Does He need letters or sounds?

No He doesn't
Of course He doesn't

Allahu Akbar!
Allahu Akbar!
Allah is greater!
Allah's speech is abound
Without needing letters or sounds
Allah is greater!

Download /stream the audio file to this book's sing-along for free!

@ itsybitsymuslims.com/singalong

About this Book

Bismillah Ar-Rahman Ar-Raheem and peace and blessings upon sayyidna Muhammad, his family, and companions.

Aqida (Islamic beliefs) is the most important and essential knowledge amongst all religious knowledges. It is the foundation of one's religion. Understanding the correct Islamic beliefs regarding Allah, His prophets, and the unseen world, is the duty of every accountable Muslim.

Aqidah linguistically is derived from the root aqada. In Arabic, one states, "aqada the rope" when the rope is tied firmly.

The manner in which the Prophet (pbuh) brought up his companions: Iman (faith) first and then the Qur'an. This is similar to what Imam Abu Hanifah pointed out; understanding the religion first and then understanding the sciences (i.e. the shari'ah). The beliefs must be corrected first, then follows all of the other aspects of the religion.

The perfect attributes of Allah are countless; however, there are 13 perfect attributes of Allah that are mentioned repeatedly in the Qur'an and by Prophet Muhammad ﷺ. Because of this, the scholars of Islam agreed unanimously that it is a personal obligation upon the accountable Muslim to know these thirteen perfect attributes.

In this book, we will be explaining the correct beliefs Muslims should have regarding the 13 perfect attributes of Allah. Our aim is to simplify the meaning of these attributes so that kids can grasp them easily.

The later scholars took special care explicitly mentioning this obligation (to know these 13 attributes), such as Sunusiyy, who is the author of the Sunusiyy Creed, which is called al Aqidah as-Sunusiyyah, and also Al Faddaliyy, and ash-Sharnubiyy (both are Maliki scholars), and others among those later scholars.

Among the heads of the scholars of the Salaf who explicitly named these attributes and indicated that it was obligatory upon every accountable muslim to know them, was Imaam Abu Hanifa. He mentioned this in his book "al Fiqhu l-Akbar".

Muslims throughout the ages taught Islamic Aqidah to children, and adults, by composing easy to understand and easy to memorize literary rhyming compositions containing the Aqidah of Muslims, according to the belief of Ahl As-sunnah wal-Jama'ah.

Here is a list and short explanation of the thirteen perfect attributes of Allah:

1. Al-Wujood - Existence: It is obligatory to believe that Allah exists and that there are no doubts about His Existence. He exists without a place and time does not lapse on Allah.

2. Al-Qidam - Being Eternal: Allah is Eternal; there is no beginning to His Existence. He has existed since before the creation.

3. Al-Baqaa' - Everlastingness: Allah is Everlasting; His existence will never come to an end. He does not perish.

4. Al-Mukhaalafah Lil-Khalq - Unlike His Creation in Any Way: Allah does not resemble His creation in absolute manner.

5. Al-Qiyaamu Bin-Nafsi - Needs No One and Nothing: Allah does not need anything or anyone from amongst His creation, but they all need Allah.

6. Al-Wahdaaniyyah - Oneness: Allah is One without any partners. He is One in His self, His attributes, and His actions.

7. Al-Hayat - Life: Allah is alive without needing a soul, skin, or heart. His Life is not similar to ours. He is alive and He never dies.

8. Al-Ilm - Knowledge: Allah's Knowledge has no limits. He know all things, even before they occur. There is nothing that Allah does not Know.

9. Al-Iradah - Will: Everything that occurs in this world happens only by the Will and decree of Allah.

10. Al-Qudrah - Power: Allah has Absolute Power over His creation.

11. As-Sama' - Hearing: Allah hears all without an ear or any other organ.

12. Al-Basar - Seeing: Allah sees all without a pupil or any other organ.

13. Al-Kalaam - Speech: Allah speaks. His speech does not require a tongue, lips, language, letters, or sounds.

This book is the first part of a three parts series explaining the essential Islamic Aqidah to Muslim children. The second part will explain the Islamic beliefs regarding the prophets, while the third part will explain the Islamic beliefs regarding things unseen, such as heavens and Angels.

We hope that these books will help your kids to learn and understand the correct Islamic beliefs, which they will need for living a fulfilling spiritual life in this world, and a happy eternal life in the final abode.

Other books by Itsy Bitsy Muslims

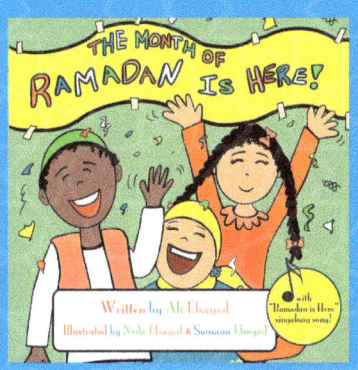

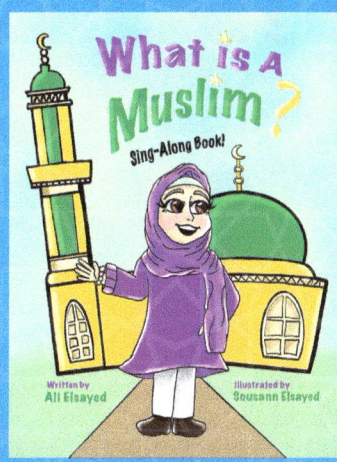

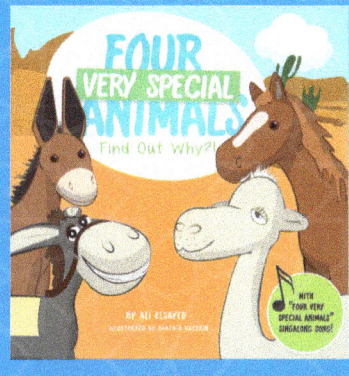

**For more children's books and sing-alongs
Visit us @Itsybitsymuslims.com**

Or scan QR code

If you purchased this book on Amazon, and you appreciate it, please leave us a positive review!

www.ingramcontent.com/pod-product-compliance
Lightning Source LLC
Chambersburg PA
CBHW050805220426
43209CB00088BA/1640